This Wedding Planner Belongs To:

____

Initial Planning Phase

IDEAS FOR THEME

IDEAS FOR VENUE

IDEAS FOR COLORS

IDEAS FOR MUSIC

IDEAS FOR RECEPTION

OTHER IDEAS

Notes & Ideas

Wedding Budget Planner

Expense MANAGER

CATEGORY/ITEMS	BUDGET	ACTUAL COST	BALANCE

Wedding Budget Checklist

CATEGORY	BUDGET	ACTUAL COST	DEPOSIT	BALANCE

Wedding Contact List

IMPORTANT VENDOR CONTACTS

	NAME	PHONE #	EMAIL	ADDRESS
OFFICIANT				
RECEPTION VENUE				
BRIDAL SHOP				
SEAMSTRESS				
FLORIST				
CATERER				
DJ/ENTERTAINMENT				
WEDDING VENUE				
TRANSPORTATION				
OTHER:				
OTHER:				
OTHER:				

NOTES & More

SPECIAL REMINDERS

Planning Snapshot

CEREMONY EXPENSE TRACKER	BUDGET	COST	DEPOSIT	BALANCE	DUE DATE
OFFICIANT GRATUITY					
MARRIAGE LICENSE					
VENUE COST					
FLOWERS					
DECORATIONS					
OTHER					

NOTES *& Reminders*

NOTES & REMINDERS

RECEPTION EXPENSE TRACKER	BUDGET	COST	DEPOSIT	BALANCE	DUE DATE
VENUE FEE					
CATERING/FOOD					
BAR/BEVERAGES					
CAKE/CUTTING FEE					
DECORATIONS					
RENTALS/EXTRAS					
BARTENDER/STAFF					

NOTES *& More*

SPECIAL REMINDERS

Planning Snapshot

PAPER PRODUCTS EXPENSE TRACKER

	BUDGET	COST	DEPOSIT	BALANCE	DUE DATE
INVITATIONS/CARDS					
POSTAGE COSTS					
THANK YOU CARDS					
PLACE CARDS					
GUESTBOOK					
OTHER					

NOTES *& Reminders*

NOTES & REMINDERS

ENTERTAINMENT EXPENSE TRACKER

	BUDGET	COST	DEPOSIT	BALANCE	DUE DATE
BAND/DJ					
SOUND SYSTEM RENTAL					
VENUE/DANCE RENTAL					
GRATUITIES					
OTHER:					
OTHER:					
OTHER:					

NOTES *& More*

SPECIAL REMINDERS

Planning Snapshot

WEDDING PARTY ATTIRE EXPENSE TRACKER

	BUDGET	COST	DEPOSIT	BALANCE	DUE DATE
WEDDING DRESS					
TUX RENTALS					
BRIDESMAID DRESSES					
SHOES/HEELS					
VEIL/GARTER/OTHER					
ALTERATION COSTS					

NOTES & Reminders

NOTES & REMINDERS

TRANSPORTATION EXPENSE TRACKER

	BUDGET	COST	DEPOSIT	BALANCE	DUE DATE
LIMO RENTAL					
VALET PARKING					
VENUE TRANSPORTATION					
AIRPORT TRANSPORTATION					
OTHER:					
OTHER:					
OTHER:					

NOTES & More

SPECIAL REMINDERS

Planning Snapshot

FLORIST EXPENSE TRACKER

	BUDGET	COST	DEPOSIT	BALANCE	DUE DATE
BOUQUETS					
VENUE DECORATIONS					
BOUTONNIERES					
VASES/EXTRAS					
TABLE DECORATIONS					
OTHER:					

NOTES & Reminders

NOTES & REMINDERS

OTHER EXPENSE TRACKER

	BUDGET	COST	DEPOSIT	BALANCE	DUE DATE
PHOTOGRAPHER					
VIDEOGRAPHER					
CATERER					
HAIR/MAKEUP/SALON					
WEDDING RINGS					
WEDDING PARTY GIFTS					
OTHER:					

NOTES & More

SPECIAL REMINDERS

Bride's Planner

HAIR APPOINTMENT

SALON NAME　　　DATE　　　TIME　　　BOOKED FOR:　　　　ADDRESS:

NOTES

MAKE UP APPOINTMENT

SALON NAME　　　DATE　　　TIME　　　BOOKED FOR:　　　　ADDRESS:

NOTES

MANICURE/PEDICURE APPOINTMENT

SALON NAME　　　DATE　　　TIME　　　BOOKED FOR:　　　　ADDRESS:

NOTES

Groom's Planner

HAIR APPOINTMENT

SALON NAME	DATE	TIME	BOOKED FOR:	ADDRESS:
			☐	
			☐	
			☐	

NOTES

TUX FITTING APPOINTMENT

BUSINESS NAME	DATE	TIME	BOOKED FOR:	ADDRESS:
			☐	
			☐	

NOTES

OTHER:

BUSINESS NAME	DATE	TIME	BOOKED FOR:	ADDRESS:
			☐	
			☐	
			☐	

NOTES

Important Dates

DATE:	DATE:	DATE:	REMINDERS
DATE:	DATE:	DATE:	
DATE:	DATE:	DATE:	
			NOTES
DATE:	DATE:	DATE:	
DATE:	DATE:	DATE:	

Weekly Wedding Planning

WEEK OF: _______________

MONDAY

TUESDAY

WEDNESDAY

THURSDAY

FRIDAY

SATURDAY

WEDDING TO DO LIST

- ☐ _______________
- ☐ _______________
- ☐ _______________
- ☐ _______________
- ☐ _______________
- ☐ _______________
- ☐ _______________
- ☐ _______________
- ☐ _______________
- ☐ _______________
- ☐ _______________
- ☐ _______________
- ☐ _______________
- ☐ _______________
- ☐ _______________
- ☐ _______________
- ☐ _______________

APPOINTMENTS & MEETINGS

DATE	TIME	VENDOR	PURPOSE

Weekly Wedding Planning

WEEK OF: ______________________

MONDAY

TUESDAY

WEDNESDAY

THURSDAY

FRIDAY

SATURDAY

WEDDING TO DO LIST

☐ _______________________
☐ _______________________
☐ _______________________
☐ _______________________
☐ _______________________
☐ _______________________
☐ _______________________
☐ _______________________
☐ _______________________
☐ _______________________
☐ _______________________
☐ _______________________
☐ _______________________

APPOINTMENTS & MEETINGS

DATE	TIME	VENDOR	PURPOSE

APPOINTMENTS & MEETINGS			
DATE	TIME	VENDOR	PURPOSE

Weekly Wedding Planning

WEEK OF:

MONDAY

TUESDAY

WEDNESDAY

THURSDAY

FRIDAY

SATURDAY

WEDDING TO DO LIST

APPOINTMENTS & MEETINGS

DATE	TIME	VENDOR	PURPOSE

Weekly Wedding Planning

WEEK OF: ___________________

MONDAY

TUESDAY

WEDNESDAY

THURSDAY

FRIDAY

SATURDAY

WEDDING TO DO LIST

APPOINTMENTS & MEETINGS

DATE	TIME	VENDOR	PURPOSE

Weekly Wedding Planning

WEEK OF:

MONDAY

TUESDAY

WEDNESDAY

THURSDAY

FRIDAY

SATURDAY

WEDDING TO DO LIST

APPOINTMENTS & MEETINGS

DATE	TIME	VENDOR	PURPOSE

Weekly Wedding Planning

WEEK OF: ___________________

MONDAY

TUESDAY

WEDNESDAY

THURSDAY

FRIDAY

SATURDAY

WEDDING TO DO LIST

- [ ] ______________________
- [ ] ______________________
- [ ] ______________________
- [ ] ______________________
- [ ] ______________________
- [ ] ______________________
- [ ] ______________________
- [ ] ______________________
- [ ] ______________________
- [ ] ______________________
- [ ] ______________________
- [ ] ______________________
- [ ] ______________________
- [ ] ______________________
- [ ] ______________________
- [ ] ______________________
- [ ] ______________________

APPOINTMENTS & MEETINGS

DATE	TIME	VENDOR	PURPOSE

Weekly Wedding Planning

WEEK OF:

MONDAY

TUESDAY

WEDNESDAY

THURSDAY

FRIDAY

SATURDAY

WEDDING TO DO LIST

APPOINTMENTS & MEETINGS

DATE	TIME	VENDOR	PURPOSE

Weekly Wedding Planning

WEEK OF: ________________

MONDAY

TUESDAY

WEDNESDAY

THURSDAY

FRIDAY

SATURDAY

WEDDING TO DO LIST

☐ ____________________
☐ ____________________
☐ ____________________
☐ ____________________
☐ ____________________
☐ ____________________
☐ ____________________
☐ ____________________
☐ ____________________
☐ ____________________
☐ ____________________
☐ ____________________
☐ ____________________
☐ ____________________
☐ ____________________
☐ ____________________
☐ ____________________

APPOINTMENTS & MEETINGS

DATE	TIME	VENDOR	PURPOSE

Weekly Wedding Planning

WEEK OF:

MONDAY

TUESDAY

WEDNESDAY

THURSDAY

FRIDAY

SATURDAY

WEDDING TO DO LIST

APPOINTMENTS & MEETINGS

DATE	TIME	VENDOR	PURPOSE

Weekly Wedding Planning

WEEK OF: _______________________

MONDAY

TUESDAY

WEDNESDAY

THURSDAY

FRIDAY

SATURDAY

WEDDING TO DO LIST

☐ _______________________
☐ _______________________
☐ _______________________
☐ _______________________
☐ _______________________
☐ _______________________
☐ _______________________
☐ _______________________
☐ _______________________
☐ _______________________
☐ _______________________
☐ _______________________
☐ _______________________
☐ _______________________
☐ _______________________
☐ _______________________
☐ _______________________
☐ _______________________

APPOINTMENTS & MEETINGS

DATE	TIME	VENDOR	PURPOSE

Weekly Wedding Planning

WEEK OF:

MONDAY

TUESDAY

WEDNESDAY

THURSDAY

FRIDAY

SATURDAY

WEDDING TO DO LIST

APPOINTMENTS & MEETINGS

DATE	TIME	VENDOR	PURPOSE

Weekly Wedding Planning

WEEK OF: ______________________

| MONDAY |
| TUESDAY |
| WEDNESDAY |
| THURSDAY |
| FRIDAY |
| SATURDAY |

WEDDING TO DO LIST

- [ ]
- [ ]
- [ ]
- [ ]
- [ ]
- [ ]
- [ ]
- [ ]
- [ ]
- [ ]
- [ ]
- [ ]
- [ ]
- [ ]
- [ ]
- [ ]

APPOINTMENTS & MEETINGS

DATE	TIME	VENDOR	PURPOSE

Weekly Wedding Planning

WEEK OF:

MONDAY

TUESDAY

WEDNESDAY

THURSDAY

FRIDAY

SATURDAY

WEDDING TO DO LIST

APPOINTMENTS & MEETINGS

DATE	TIME	VENDOR	PURPOSE

Weekly Wedding Planning

WEEK OF: _______________

MONDAY

TUESDAY

WEDNESDAY

THURSDAY

FRIDAY

SATURDAY

WEDDING TO DO LIST

- [ ]
- [ ]
- [ ]
- [ ]
- [ ]
- [ ]
- [ ]
- [ ]
- [ ]
- [ ]
- [ ]
- [ ]
- [ ]
- [ ]
- [ ]
- [ ]

APPOINTMENTS & MEETINGS

DATE	TIME	VENDOR	PURPOSE

Weekly Wedding Planning

WEEK OF:

MONDAY

TUESDAY

WEDNESDAY

THURSDAY

FRIDAY

SATURDAY

WEDDING TO DO LIST

APPOINTMENTS & MEETINGS

DATE	TIME	VENDOR	PURPOSE

Weekly Wedding Planning

WEEK OF: ___________

MONDAY

TUESDAY

WEDNESDAY

THURSDAY

FRIDAY

SATURDAY

WEDDING TO DO LIST

APPOINTMENTS & MEETINGS

DATE	TIME	VENDOR	PURPOSE

Weekly Wedding Planning

WEEK OF:

MONDAY

TUESDAY

WEDNESDAY

THURSDAY

FRIDAY

SATURDAY

WEDDING TO DO LIST

APPOINTMENTS & MEETINGS

DATE	TIME	VENDOR	PURPOSE

Weekly Wedding Planning

WEEK OF: _______________

MONDAY

TUESDAY

WEDNESDAY

THURSDAY

FRIDAY

SATURDAY

WEDDING TO DO LIST

APPOINTMENTS & MEETINGS

DATE	TIME	VENDOR	PURPOSE

Weekly Wedding Planning

WEEK OF:

MONDAY

TUESDAY

WEDNESDAY

THURSDAY

FRIDAY

SATURDAY

WEDDING TO DO LIST

- [ ]
- [ ]
- [ ]
- [ ]
- [ ]
- [ ]
- [ ]
- [ ]
- [ ]
- [ ]
- [ ]
- [ ]
- [ ]
- [ ]

APPOINTMENTS & MEETINGS

DATE	TIME	VENDOR	PURPOSE

Wedding Planner

12 Months BEFORE WEDDING

- PLANNING GUIDELINE -

SET THE DATE	CONSIDER FLORISTS	CONSIDER MUSIC CHOICES
SET YOUR BUDGET	RESEARCH CATERERS	DECIDE ON OFFICIANT
CONSIDER WEDDING THEMES	DECIDE ON OFFICIANT	CONSIDER TRANSPORTATION
PLAN ENGAGEMENT PARTY	CREATE INITIAL GUEST LIST	CREATE INITIAL GUEST LIST
RESEARCH POSSIBLE VENUES	CHOOSE WEDDING PARTY	CHOOSE WEDDING PARTY
START RESEARCHING GOWNS	CONSIDER ACCESSORIES	BRIDEMAIDS GOWNS
RESEARCH PHOTOGRAPHERS	REGISTER WITH GIFT REGISTRY	BOOK TENTATIVE HOTELS
RESEARCH VIDEOGRAPHERS	DISCUSS HONEYMOON IDEAS	CONSIDER BEAUTY SALONS
RESEARCH DJS/ENTERTAINMENT	RESEARCH WEDDING RINGS	CONSIDER SHOES & OTHER

Things To Do   Status

TOP PRIORITIES

NOTES & IDEAS

APPOINTMENTS & REMINDERS

Wedding Planner

- PLANNING GUIDELINE -

FINALIZE GUEST LIST

ORDER INVITATIONS

PLAN YOUR RECEPTION

BOOK PHOTOGRAPHER

BOOK VIDEOGRAPHER

CHOOSE WEDDING GOWN

ORDER BRIDESMAIDS DRESSES

RESERVE TUXEDOS

ARRANGE TRANSPORTATION

BOOK WEDDING VENUE

BOOK RECEPTION VENUE

PLAN HONEYMOON

BOOK FLORIST

BOOK DJ/ENTERTAINMENT

BOOK CATERER

CHOOSE WEDDING CAKE

BOOK OFFICIANT

BOOK ROOMS FOR GUESTS

Things To Do   Status

TOP PRIORITIES

NOTES & IDEAS

APPOINTMENTS & REMINDERS

Wedding Planner

6 *Months* BEFORE WEDDING

- PLANNING GUIDELINE -

ORDER THANK YOU NOTES

REVIEW RECEPTION DETAILS

MAKE APPT FOR FITTING

CONFIRM BRIDAL DRESSES

OBTAIN MARRIAGE LICENSE

BOOK HAIR STYLIST

BOOK NAIL SALON

CONFIRM MUSIC SELECTION

WRITE VOWS

PLAN BRIDAL SHOWER

PLAN REHEARSAL

BOOK REHEARSAL DINNER

SHOP FOR WEDDING RINGS

PLAN DECORATIONS

CHOOSE BOUQUET TYPE

FINALIZE GUEST LIST

UPDATE PASSPORTS

CONFIRM HOTEL ROOMS

Things To Do   Status

TOP PRIORITIES

NOTES & IDEAS

APPOINTMENTS & REMINDERS

Wedding Planner

- PLANNING GUIDELINE -

MAIL OUT INVITATIONS	FINALIZE HONEYMOON PLANS	CONFIRM CATERER
MEET WITH OFFICIANT	ATTEND FIRST DRESS FITTING	FINALIZE RING FITTING
BUY WEDDING FAVORS	FINALIZE VOWS	CONFIRM FLOWERS
BUY WEDDING PARTY GIFTS	FINALIZE RECEPTION MENU	CONFIRM BAND
PURCHASE SHOES	KEEP TRACK OF RSVPS	SHOP FOR HONEYMOON
FINALIZE THANK YOU CARDS	BOOK PHOTO SESSION	BUY GARTER BELT

Things To Do   Status

TOP PRIORITIES

NOTES & IDEAS

APPOINTMENTS & REMINDERS

Wedding Planner

- PLANNING GUIDELINE -

- CHOOSE YOUR MC
- REQUEST SPECIAL TOASTS
- ARRANGE TRANSPORTATION
- CHOOSE YOUR HAIR STYLE
- CHOOSE YOUR NAIL COLOR
- ATTEND BRIDAL SHOWER

- CONFIRM CAKE CHOICES
- CONFIRM MENU (FINAL)
- CONFIRM SEATING
- CONFIRM VIDEOGRAPHER
- ARRANGE LEGAL DOCS
- FINALIZE WEDDING DUTIES

- CONFIRM BRIDESMAID DRESSES
- MEET WITH DJ/MC
- FINAL DRESS FITTING
- WRAP WEDDIING PARTY GIFTS
- CONFIRM FINAL GUEST COUNT
- CREATE WEDDING SCHEDULE

Things To Do   Status

TOP PRIORITIES

NOTES & IDEAS

APPOINTMENTS & REMINDERS

Wedding Planner

1 *Week* BEFORE WEDDING

- PLANNING GUIDELINE -

- PAYMENT TO VENDORS
- PACK FOR HONEYMOON
- CONFIRM HOTEL RESERVATION
- GIVE SCHEDULE TO PARTY
- DELIVER LICENSE TO OFFICIANT
- CONFIRM WITH VENDORS

- PICK UP WEDDING DRESS
- PICK UP TUXEDOS
- GIVE MUSIC LIST TO DJ/BAND
- CONFIRM SHOES/HEELS FIT
- CONFIRM TRANSPORTATION
- MONEY FOR GRATUITIES

- COMPLETE MAKE UP TRIAL
- CONFIRM RINGS FIT
- CONFIRM TRAVEL PLANS
- CONFIRM HOTELS FOR GUESTS
- OTHER:
- OTHER:

Things To Do   Status

TOP PRIORITIES

NOTES & IDEAS

APPOINTMENTS & REMINDERS

Wedding Planner

- PLANNING GUIDELINE -

1 Day BEFORE WEDDING

ATTEND REHEARSAL DINNER

FINISH HONEYMOON PACKING

GREET OUT OF TOWN GUESTS

GET MANICURE/PEDICURE

CHECK ON WEDDING VENUE

CHECK WEATHER TO PREPARE

GIVE GIFTS TO WEDDING PARTY

CONFIRM RINGS FIT

GET A GOOD NIGHT'S SLEEP

Things To Do | Status

TOP PRIORITIES

NOTES & IDEAS

APPOINTMENTS & REMINDERS

Your Special Day!

Day of WEDDING

GET YOUR HAIR DONE

GET YOUR MAKE UP DONE

HAVE A LIGHT BREAKFAST

MEET WITH BRIDAL PARTY

GIVE RINGS TO BEST MAN

ENJOY YOUR SPECIAL DAY!

Wedding Attire Planner

WEDDING ATTIRE EXPENSE TRACKER

ITEM/PURCHASE	STATUS ✓	DATE PAID	TOTAL COST

NOTES & REMINDERS	
	TOTAL COST:

Notes:

WEDDING ATTIRE DETAILS

Venue Planner

VENUE EXPENSE TRACKER

ITEM/PURCHASE	STATUS ✔	DATE PAID	TOTAL COST

NOTES & REMINDERS

TOTAL COST:

Notes:

VENUE PLANNING DETAILS

Catering Planner

CATERING EXPENSE TRACKER

ITEM/PURCHASE	STATUS ✓	DATE PAID	TOTAL COST

NOTES & REMINDERS

TOTAL COST:

Notes:

CATERING PLANNER DETAILS

Entertainment Planner

ENTERTAINMENT EXPENSE TRACKER

ITEM/PURCHASE	STATUS ✓	DATE PAID	TOTAL COST

NOTES & REMINDERS

TOTAL COST:

Notes:

Love

ENTERTAINMENT DETAILS

Videographer Planner

VIDEOGRAPHER EXPENSE TRACKER

ITEM/PURCHASE	STATUS ✓	DATE PAID	TOTAL COST

NOTES & REMINDERS

TOTAL COST:

Notes:

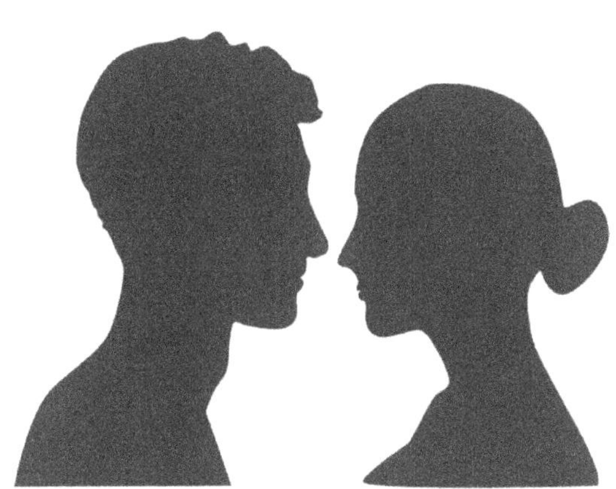

VIDEOGRAPHER DETAILS

Photographer Planner

PHOTOGRAPHER EXPENSE TRACKER

ITEM/PURCHASE	STATUS ✓	DATE PAID	TOTAL COST

NOTES & REMINDERS

TOTAL COST:

Notes:

PHOTOGRAPHER DETAILS

Florist Planner

ITEM/PURCHASE	STATUS ✓	DATE PAID	TOTAL COST

NOTES & REMINDERS

TOTAL COST:

Notes:

FLORIST PLANNING DETAILS

Extra Wedding Costs

MISC WEDDING EXPENSE TRACKER

ITEM/PURCHASE	STATUS ✓	DATE PAID	TOTAL COST

NOTES & REMINDERS

TOTAL COST:

Notes:

MISC WEDDING DETAILS

Bachelorette Party Planner

EVENT DETAILS

DATE

TIME

VENUE

THEME

HOST

OTHER

SCHEDULE OF EVENTS

TIME	

GUEST LIST

FIRST NAME	LAST NAME	R

SUPPLIES & SHOPPING LIST

- [ ]
- [ ]
- [ ]
- [ ]
- [ ]
- [ ]
- [ ]
- [ ]
- [ ]
- [ ]
- [ ]
- [ ]
- [ ]
- [ ]

NOTES & REMINDERS

love

Bachelor Party Planner

EVENT DETAILS

DATE

TIME

VENUE

THEME

HOST

OTHER

SCHEDULE OF EVENTS

TIME

GUEST LIST

FIRST NAME	LAST NAME	R

SUPPLIES & SHOPPING LIST

NOTES & REMINDERS

love

Reception Planner

HORS D'OEUVRES

1st COURSE:

3rd COURSE:

2nd COURSE:

4th COURSE:

MEAL PLANNING NOTES

Wedding Planning Notes

IDEAS & REMINDERS

Wedding to do List

Wedding Guest List

NAME	ADDRESS	PHONE #	# IN PARTY	RSVP: ✓

Wedding Guest List

NAME	ADDRESS	PHONE #	# IN PARTY	RSVP: ✓

Wedding Guest List

NAME	ADDRESS	PHONE #	# IN PARTY	RSVP: ✓

Wedding Guest List

NAME	ADDRESS	PHONE #	# IN PARTY	RSVP: ✓

Wedding Guest List

NAME	ADDRESS	PHONE #	# IN PARTY	RSVP: ✓

Wedding Guest List

NAME	ADDRESS	PHONE #	# IN PARTY	RSVP: ✓

Wedding Guest List

NAME	ADDRESS	PHONE #	# IN PARTY	RSVP: ✓

Wedding Guest List

NAME	ADDRESS	PHONE #	# IN PARTY	RSVP: ✓

Wedding Guest List

NAME	ADDRESS	PHONE #	# IN PARTY	RSVP: ✓

Wedding Guest List

NAME	ADDRESS	PHONE #	# IN PARTY	RSVP: ✓

Wedding Seating Chart

Table #

TABLE #:

1:

2:

3:

4:

5:

6:

7:

8:

love

Table #

TABLE #:

1:

2:

3:

4:

5:

6:

7:

8:

Wedding Seating Chart

Table #

TABLE #:

1 :

2 :

3 :

4 :

5 :

6 :

7 :

8 :

Table #

TABLE #:

1 :

2 :

3 :

4 :

5 :

6 :

7 :

8 :

Wedding Seating Chart

Table #

TABLE #:

1:

2:

3:

4:

5:

6:

7:

8:

Table #

TABLE #:

1:

2:

3:

4:

5:

6:

7:

8:

Wedding Seating Chart

Table #

TABLE #:

1:

2:

3:

4:

5:

6:

7:

8:

Table #

TABLE #:

1:

2:

3:

4:

5:

6:

7:

8:

Wedding Seating Chart

Table #

TABLE #:

1:

2:

3:

4:

5:

6:

7:

8:

Table #

TABLE #:

1:

2:

3:

4:

5:

6:

7:

8:

Wedding Seating Chart

Table #

TABLE #:

1:

2:

3:

4:

5:

6:

7:

8:

Table #

TABLE #:

1:

2:

3:

4:

5:

6:

7:

8:

Wedding Seating Chart

Table #

<table>
<tr><td>TABLE #:</td></tr>
<tr><td>1:</td></tr>
<tr><td>2:</td></tr>
<tr><td>3:</td></tr>
<tr><td>4:</td></tr>
<tr><td>5:</td></tr>
<tr><td>6:</td></tr>
<tr><td>7:</td></tr>
<tr><td>8:</td></tr>
</table>

Table #

<table>
<tr><td>TABLE #:</td></tr>
<tr><td>1:</td></tr>
<tr><td>2:</td></tr>
<tr><td>3:</td></tr>
<tr><td>4:</td></tr>
<tr><td>5:</td></tr>
<tr><td>6:</td></tr>
<tr><td>7:</td></tr>
<tr><td>8:</td></tr>
</table>

Wedding Seating Chart

Table #

TABLE #:

1:

2:

3:

4:

5:

6:

7:

8:

Table #

TABLE #:

1:

2:

3:

4:

5:

6:

7:

8:

Wedding Seating Chart

Table #

TABLE #:

1:

2:

3:

4:

5:

6:

7:

8:

Table #

TABLE #:

1:

2:

3:

4:

5:

6:

7:

8:

Wedding Seating Chart

Table #

TABLE #:

1:

2:

3:

4:

5:

6:

7:

8:

Table #

TABLE #:

1:

2:

3:

4:

5:

6:

7:

8:

Wedding Seating Chart

Table #

TABLE #:

1:

2:

3:

4:

5:

6:

7:

8:

Table #

TABLE #:

1:

2:

3:

4:

5:

6:

7:

8:

Wedding Seating Chart

Table #

<table>
<tr><td>TABLE #:</td></tr>
<tr><td>1:</td></tr>
<tr><td>2:</td></tr>
<tr><td>3:</td></tr>
<tr><td>4:</td></tr>
<tr><td>5:</td></tr>
<tr><td>6:</td></tr>
<tr><td>7:</td></tr>
<tr><td>8:</td></tr>
</table>

Table #

<table>
<tr><td>TABLE #:</td></tr>
<tr><td>1:</td></tr>
<tr><td>2:</td></tr>
<tr><td>3:</td></tr>
<tr><td>4:</td></tr>
<tr><td>5:</td></tr>
<tr><td>6:</td></tr>
<tr><td>7:</td></tr>
<tr><td>8:</td></tr>
</table>

Wedding Seating Chart

Table #

TABLE #:

1:

2:

3:

4:

5:

6:

7:

8:

Table #

TABLE #:

1:

2:

3:

4:

5:

6:

7:

8:

Wedding Seating Chart

Table #

TABLE #:

1:

2:

3:

4:

5:

6:

7:

8:

Table #

TABLE #:

1:

2:

3:

4:

5:

6:

7:

8:

Wedding Seating Chart

Table #

TABLE #:

1:

2:

3:

4:

5:

6:

7:

8:

Table #

TABLE #:

1:

2:

3:

4:

5:

6:

7:

8:

Wedding Seating Chart

Table #

Table #

Wedding Seating Chart

Table #

TABLE #:

1:

2:

3:

4:

5:

6:

7:

8:

Table #

TABLE #:

1:

2:

3:

4:

5:

6:

7:

8:

Wedding Seating Chart

Table #

<table>
<tr><td>TABLE #:</td></tr>
<tr><td>1:</td></tr>
<tr><td>2:</td></tr>
<tr><td>3:</td></tr>
<tr><td>4:</td></tr>
<tr><td>5:</td></tr>
<tr><td>6:</td></tr>
<tr><td>7:</td></tr>
<tr><td>8:</td></tr>
</table>

Table #

<table>
<tr><td>TABLE #:</td></tr>
<tr><td>1:</td></tr>
<tr><td>2:</td></tr>
<tr><td>3:</td></tr>
<tr><td>4:</td></tr>
<tr><td>5:</td></tr>
<tr><td>6:</td></tr>
<tr><td>7:</td></tr>
<tr><td>8:</td></tr>
</table>

Wedding Seating Chart

Table

TABLE #:

1:

2:

3:

4:

5:

6:

7:

8:

Table

TABLE #:

1:

2:

3:

4:

5:

6:

7:

8:

Wedding Seating Chart

Table #

TABLE #:

1:

2:

3:

4:

5:

6:

7:

8:

Table #

TABLE #:

1:

2:

3:

4:

5:

6:

7:

8:

Wedding Seating Chart

Table #

TABLE #:

1:

2:

3:

4:

5:

6:

7:

8:

Table #

TABLE #:

1:

2:

3:

4:

5:

6:

7:

8:

Wedding Seating Chart

Table #

TABLE #:

1:

2:

3:

4:

5:

6:

7:

8:

Table #

TABLE #:

1:

2:

3:

4:

5:

6:

7:

8:

Wedding Seating Chart

Table #

TABLE #:

1:

2:

3:

4:

5:

6:

7:

8:

Table #

TABLE #:

1:

2:

3:

4:

5:

6:

7:

8:

Wedding Seating Chart

Table #

TABLE #:

1:

2:

3:

4:

5:

6:

7:

8:

Table #

TABLE #:

1:

2:

3:

4:

5:

6:

7:

8:

Wedding Seating Chart

Table #

TABLE #:

1:

2:

3:

4:

5:

6:

7:

8:

Table #

TABLE #:

1:

2:

3:

4:

5:

6:

7:

8:

Wedding Seating Chart

Table #

TABLE #:

1:

2:

3:

4:

5:

6:

7:

8:

Table #

TABLE #:

1:

2:

3:

4:

5:

6:

7:

8:

Wedding Seating Chart

Table #

TABLE #:

1: 2: 3: 4: 5: 6: 7: 8:

9: 10: 11: 12: 13: 14: 15: 16:

Table #

TABLE #:

1: 2: 3: 4: 5: 6: 7: 8:

9: 10: 11: 12: 13: 14: 15: 16:

Wedding Seating Chart

Table #

TABLE #:

1:          2:   3:   4:   5:   6:   7:   8:

9:          10:   11:   12:   13:   14:   15:   16:

Table #

TABLE #:

1:          2:   3:   4:   5:   6:   7:   8:

9:          10:   11:   12:   13:   14:   15:   16:

Wedding Seating Chart

Table #

TABLE #:

1:	2:	3:	4:	5:	6:	7:	8:
9:	10:	11:	12:	13:	14:	15:	16:

Table #

TABLE #:

1:	2:	3:	4:	5:	6:	7:	8:
9:	10:	11:	12:	13:	14:	15:	16:

Wedding Seating Chart

Table

TABLE #:

1:	2:	3:	4:	5:	6:	7:	8:
9:	10:	11:	12:	13:	14:	15:	16:

Table

TABLE #:

1:	2:	3:	4:	5:	6:	7:	8:
9:	10:	11:	12:	13:	14:	15:	16:

Wedding Seating Chart

Table #

TABLE #:

1:	2:	3:	4:	5:	6:	7:	8:
9:	10:	11:	12:	13:	14:	15:	16:

Table #

TABLE #:

1:	2:	3:	4:	5:	6:	7:	8:
9:	10:	11:	12:	13:	14:	15:	16:

Wedding Seating Chart

Table

TABLE #:

1:	2:	3:	4:	5:	6:	7:	8:
9:	10:	11:	12:	13:	14:	15:	16:

Table

TABLE #:

1:	2:	3:	4:	5:	6:	7:	8:
9:	10:	11:	12:	13:	14:	15:	16:

Wedding Seating Chart

Table

TABLE #:

1:	2:	3:	4:	5:	6:	7:	8:
9:	10:	11:	12:	13:	14:	15:	16:

Table

TABLE #:

1:	2:	3:	4:	5:	6:	7:	8:
9:	10:	11:	12:	13:	14:	15:	16:

Wedding Seating Chart

Table #

TABLE #:

1:	2:	3:	4:	5:	6:	7:	8:
9:	10:	11:	12:	13:	14:	15:	16:

Table #

TABLE #:

1:	2:	3:	4:	5:	6:	7:	8:
9:	10:	11:	12:	13:	14:	15:	16:

Wedding Seating Chart

Table

TABLE #:

1:	2:	3:	4:	5:	6:	7:	8:
9:	10:	11:	12:	13:	14:	15:	16:

Table

TABLE #:

1:	2:	3:	4:	5:	6:	7:	8:
9:	10:	11:	12:	13:	14:	15:	16:

Wedding Seating Chart

Table

TABLE #:

1:	2:	3:	4:	5:	6:	7:	8:
9:	10:	11:	12:	13:	14:	15:	16:

Table

TABLE #:

1:	2:	3:	4:	5:	6:	7:	8:
9:	10:	11:	12:	13:	14:	15:	16:

Wedding Seating Chart

Table #

TABLE #:

1:	2:	3:	4:	5:	6:	7:	8:
9:	10:	11:	12:	13:	14:	15:	16:

Table #

TABLE #:

1:	2:	3:	4:	5:	6:	7:	8:
9:	10:	11:	12:	13:	14:	15:	16: